A Little Book of

A Little Book of

Beauty

Ruskin Bond

SPEAKING
TIGER

SPEAKING TIGER PUBLISHING PVT. LTD
4381/4 Ansari Road, Daryaganj,
New Delhi–110002, India

ISBN: 978-93-87693-74-6
eISBN: 978-93-87693-73-9

10 9 8 7 6 5 4 3 2 1

Typeset in Garamond Pro by SÜRYA, New Delhi
Printed at Thomson Press, Delhi

Introduction

Beauty needs no introduction (so I'll keep this short!)—either it's there, or it isn't. Either you see it, or you don't.

The other day I came across the word 'pulchritude'. As it meant nothing to me, I looked it up in my little Oxford English Dictionary and discovered, to my surprise, that it meant 'beauty'. Not a very beautiful word. I would hesitate to go up to a beautiful woman and say, 'I am bowled over by your pulchritude.' I would probably be bowled over by a thump on the head from her handbag.

Even the word 'beautiful' is one that I rarely use. It implies perfection, and that is not my idea of beauty, as it excludes all of humanity, a perfect riot of imperfections. It is said that god made man in his own image. Well, he must have been distracted during the process because there is not a lot that is god-like about the human species. Yes, we have made beautiful music, beautiful paintings, beautiful poems, but we have also created nuclear bombs, poisonous gases, poisonous ideas, plastic and toxic waste. A degraded world.

It is nature that gives us true beauty—the celestial bodies, rivers, seas and mountains; a new leaf, a flower in bloom, a blade of grass, a seed. Above all, a seed! We have turned our backs on Nature and gone instead for a plastic world. Plastic flowers last longer, don't they? And some might find them beautiful. (But if it makes them happier and kinder people, I should not complain.)

We have been doing our best to make beauty a rather meaningless word. Beauty queens and their male counterparts conform to a set pattern, to formulae that change from time to time but remain plastic and impersonal. Models who launch a thousand products must smile, but not with their hearts; only to reveal perfect, gleaming white teeth for us to marvel at.

The same teeth in a skeleton would not look beautiful.

So beauty lies in the mind of the beholder. Not everyone has a beautiful mind, but that is another story…

And there are many kinds of beauty. An affluent tourist was admiring the sunset over a mountain range. The villager standing beside him had seen it every day. 'It doesn't fill my family's stomachs,' he said, and returned to hoeing his barren fields. For him, green-gold shoots of paddy and wheat are far more beautiful.

Yes, there are many kinds of beauty—as many as there are eyes to see and hearts to feel. Like the writers collected in this little book, you will have your own ideas of beauty; your own sightings of it. Write them down in the pages provided for your notes. You might surprise yourself!

Ruskin Bond
Landour, May 2018

(Publisher's note: All quotes in the book that are not attributed to anyone are by Ruskin Bond.)

Azure butterflies flit about
  the garden like flakes of sky...
When all the wars are done,
  a butterfly will still be beautiful.

April on my hill: wild roses in
flower—small white blossoms
lying in clusters; pink and blue
primroses on the green slopes;
and liquid sunshine, like honey.

At night, a young breeze sings
in the oaks, where the
king crows come to sleep.

.Ruskin Bond.

The sky is translucent
When the rain is done,
And the moon, free from the
    web of clouds
Has lifted the veil of darkness.
Behold the night of autumn,
    starred and gentle,
Garbed in the spotless
    fabric of moonlight.

—*Kalidasa (tr. K.S. Pandit)*

❧

The poetry of the earth is never dead.

—*John Keats*

❧

There's beauty in the sight of things, in the sound of things. And in the clear mountain air, there's beauty in the smell of things.

❧

Never say there is nothing beautiful in the world anymore. There is always something to make you wonder in the shape of a tree, the trembling of a leaf.

—*Albert Schweitzer*

❧

What more perfect song, Lord,
  than the songbird
  at dawn's first light;
What lovelier thing than the
  ladybird opening
  its wings on a rose;
What higher grace than work-worn
  hands rocking
  an infant to sleep.

I said to the almond tree, 'Sister,
speak to me of God,' and the
almond tree blossomed.
  —*Nikos Kazantzakis*

Beauty surrounds us.

—*Rumi*

The mind can go in a thousand directions, but on this beautiful path, I walk in peace. With each step, the wind blows. With each step, a flower blooms.

—*Thich Nhat Hanh*

Though we travel the world over to find the beautiful, we must carry it with us or we find it not.

—*Ralph Waldo Emerson*

Wherever we arrive with an open heart, *there* is beauty.

Those who live in towns should carefully remember this, for their own sakes...for their children's sakes: Never lose an opportunity of seeing anything beautiful. Beauty is God's handwriting—a way-side sacrament; welcome it in every fair face, every fair sky, every fair flower, and thank for it Him, the fountain of all loveliness, and drink it in, simply and earnestly, with all your eyes; it is a charmed draught, a cup of blessing.

—*Charles Kingsley*

Notes

_____

_____

_____

_____

_____

_____

_____

_____

_____

_____

_____

_____

.17.

.A Little Book of Beauty.

.18.

——————————————
——————————————
——————————————
——————————————
——————————————
——————————————
——————————————
——————————————
——————————————
——————————————
——————————————
——————————————
——————————————
——————————————
——————————————
——————————————
——————————————
——————————————

.Ruskin Bond.

_____

_____

_____

_____

_____

_____

_____

_____

_____

_____   *.19.*

_____

_____

_____

_____

_____

_____

_____

❧

.20.

_____
_____
_____
_____
_____
_____
_____
_____
_____
_____
_____
_____
_____
_____
_____
_____

.Ruskin Bond.

There is nothing you can see
that is not a flower;
There is nothing you can think
that is not the moon.

—Matsuo Basho(tr. Reginald Blyth)

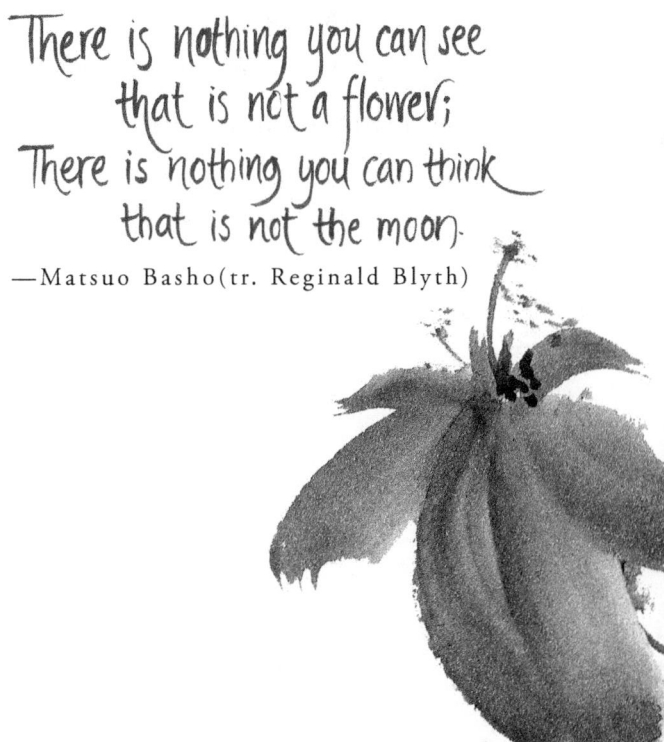

A Late lark twitters from the
    quiet skies;
And from the west,
Where the sun, his day's work
    ended,
Lingers as in content,
There falls on the old, gray city
An influence luminous and serene,
A shining peace.

—*William Ernest Henley*

❧

The sun has set. I watch the owlets emerge from their holes in the trees, spread their short, rounded wings and sail off for the night's hunting. Silence descends. Only the shuffling of porcupines, the soft flip-flop of moths beating against the window panes. The power goes off. A yellow moon blooms above the hill.

Everything in the world is
beautiful, but Man only
recognizes beauty if he sees
it either seldom or from afar.
Listen, today we are gods! Our
blue shadows are enormous! We
move in a gigantic, joyful world!
—*Vladimir Nabokov*

The most beautiful adventures are
not those we go to seek.
—*Robert Louis Stevenson*

.Ruskin Bond.

A man should hear a little music, read a little poetry, and see a fine picture every day of his life, in order that worldly cares may not obliterate the sense of the beautiful which God has implanted in the human soul.

—*Johann Wolfgang von Goethe*

❧

Stop and smell the roses.

—*Anonymous*

❧

A thing of beauty is a joy for ever:
Its loveliness increases; it will never
Pass into nothingness; but still
   will keep
A bower quiet for us, and a sleep
Full of sweet dreams, and health,
   and quiet breathing.
—*John Keats*

❦

The mountains brood massively under a darkening sky. All is still. Then, emerging from the depths of the forest like a dark, sweet secret comes the indescribably beautiful call of the whistling thrush.

Sunshine after days of rain. Whistling thrush perched on the broken garden fence—silent, but a glistening, fragile deep purple.

I have an idea that the only thing which makes it possible to regard this world we live in without disgust is the beauty which now and then men create out of the chaos. The pictures they paint, the music they compose, the books they write, and the lives they lead. Of all these the richest in beauty is the beautiful life. That is the perfect work of art.

—*W. Somerset Maugham*

Notes

_____

_____

_____

_____

_____

_____

_____

_____

_____

_____

_____

_____

.30.

.Ruskin Bond.

_____

_____

_____

_____

_____

_____

_____

_____

_____

_____   *.31.*

_____

_____

_____

_____

_____

_____

_____

🌱

.32.

_____
_____
_____
_____
_____
_____
_____
_____
_____
_____
_____
_____
_____
_____
_____
_____
_____

❧

And the dawn broke
Rose-pink behind the mountains
And the river ran silver and gold.

From the little brook at the bottom of the hill, the constant music of water—a murmur in my room, a soft chatter when I go down and sit close to it.

The beauty of a quiet, enduring companionship.

.Ruskin Bond.

The gift of friendship is always
beautiful, given or received.

❧

Beauty is gentle, and only the
gentle receive its benediction. Eyes
that look in anger only see ugliness
and desolation.

❧

To see a World in a grain of sand
And a Heaven in a wild flower
Hold infinity in the palm of your
hand
And eternity in an hour.

—*William Blake*

Think of all the beauty still left
around you and be happy.

—*Anne Frank*

The appearance of things changes according to the emotions; and thus we see magic and beauty in them, while the magic and beauty are really in ourselves.

—*Kahlil Gibran*

Beauty is no quality in things themselves: It exists merely in the mind which contemplates them; and each mind perceives a different beauty.

—*David Hume*

A human being is a part of the whole called by us Universe, a part limited in time and space. He experiences himself, his thoughts and feelings, as something separated from the rest, a kind of optical delusion of his consciousness. This delusion is a prison for us, restricting us to our personal desires and to affection for a few persons nearest to us. Our task must be to free ourselves from this prison by widening our circle of compassion to embrace all living creatures, and the whole of nature in its beauty.

—*Albert Einstein*

Some choose to sail around the world in boats and aeroplanes, chasing beauty and new experience. Others remain in their own patch, yet see the world in a grain of sand.

There are nettles everywhere, but smooth, green grasses are more common still; the blue of heaven is larger than the cloud.

—*Elizabeth Barrett Browning*

A mountain summer, long ago.
I spent a night on the pine knoll
below my cottage, stretched
out on the grass beneath my
favourite cherry tree. I lay awake
for hours, listening to the chink
and burble of a stream, the
singing of crickets, the occasional
chuckle of some night bird;
and watching, through the
branches overhead, the stars, like
overlapping diamonds in the
immensity of sky.

❧

.Ruskin Bond.

Notes

_____

_____

_____

_____

_____

_____

_____

_____

_____

_____

_____

_____

❧

.42.

❧

.Ruskin Bond.

_____

_____

_____

_____

_____

_____

_____

_____

_____   *.43.*

_____

_____

_____

_____

_____

_____

_____

_____

🌿

.44.

.Ruskin Bond.

Dwell on the beauty of life.
Watch the stars, and see yourself
running with them.

—Marcus Aurelius

You ask me why I live on the
green mountain.
I smile, I don't answer, my heart
is at rest.
Peach blossoms are carried far by
flowing water,
Here, apart, I have both heaven
and earth.

—Li Bai (tr. Sarah Beck)

Almost always, it is the unexpected that delights us, that takes us by the throat and gives us a good shaking, leaving us gasping in wonder. It may only be a shaft of sunlight slanting through the pillars of an old banyan tree, or dewdrops caught in a spider's web, or in the stillness of the mountains, the sudden chatter of a little stream as you round the bend of a hill.

❧

Scenery is fine—but human
nature is finer.

—*John Keats*

Sweet are the pleasures that to
verse belong,
And doubly sweet a brotherhood
in song.

—*John Keats*

Beauty ought to look a little surprised: it is the emotion that best suits her face, as Botticelli knew when he painted her risen from the waves, between the winds and the flowers. The beauty who does not look surprised, who accepts her position as her due— she reminds us too much of a prima donna.

—*E.M. Forster*

It is true that the mind is a great gift, but the body is not to be scorned, either.

In the crooks of your body, I find my religion.

—*Sappho*

To find beauty in ugliness is the province of the poet.

—*Thomas Hardy*

🌿

If everyone were not so indolent they would realize that beauty is beauty even when it is irritating, and stimulating not only when it is accepted and classic.

—*Gertrude Stein*

🌿

Beauty is indeed a good gift of God; but that the good may not think it a great good, God dispenses it even to the wicked.

—*St Augustine*

Beauty is how you feel inside, and it reflects in your eyes. It is not something physical.

—*Sophia Loren*

Notes

_____
_____
_____
_____
_____
_____
_____
_____
_____
_____
_____
_____
_____
_____

❧

.54.

.Ruskin Bond.

_____

_____

_____

_____

_____

_____

_____

_____

_____   .55.

_____

_____

_____

_____

_____

_____

_____

❧

.Ruskin Bond.

It has bloomed again,
The flower I'd thought dead.

Beauty is but the sensible image of the Infinite. Like truth and justice it lives within us; like virtue and the moral law it is a companion of the soul.

—*George Bancroft*

The contemplation of beauty causes the soul to grow wings.

—*Plato*

Beauty, like love and happiness, multiplies when it is shared. And there is a lot more to sharing than exchanging photographs of beautiful places.

❧

Far better to take someone to the garden than to uproot a tender flowering plant to give them.

❧

In every person there is a sun.
Just let them shine.

—*Socrates*

There is beauty in giving, and
expecting nothing in return.

The beauty of appearance only appears so.

✥

The question is not what you look at, but what you see.

—*Henry David Thoreau*

✥

The fairest thing in nature, a flower, still has its roots in earth and manure.

—*D.H. Lawrence*

Beauty is an experience, nothing else. It is not a fixed pattern or an arrangement of features. It is something felt, a glow or a communicated sense of fineness.

—*D.H. Lawrence*

When they smile, whom blind
fate has given no reason to smile,
it is a miracle of beauty that
would shame the gods.

❧

I can't help feeling that there is no
beauty without hope, struggle, and
victory.

—*Luis Bunuel*

❧

the river is a black mirror at night
and the quarter moon and the
    half moon
sail on her and within her by
    turns—
lamp-lit boats, dream-lit boats
that move with the river's
    endless dreaming.
              —*Keki Daruwalla*

Notes

_____
_____
_____
_____
_____
_____
_____
_____
_____
_____
_____
_____
_____
_____

❧

.66.

.Ruskin Bond.

_____

_____

_____

_____

_____

_____

_____

_____

_____

_____   *.67.*

_____

_____

_____

_____

_____

_____

_____

❧

.68.

.Ruskin Bond.

There are as many styles of beauty
as there are versions of happiness.

—Stendhal

I seek truth and beauty in the transparency of an autumn leaf, in the perfect form of a seashell on the beach, in the curve of a woman's back, in the texture of an ancient tree trunk, but also in the elusive forms of reality.

—*Isabel Allende*

The universe is full of magical things patiently waiting for our wits to grow sharper.

—*Eden Phillpotts*

❧

Through our eyes, the universe is perceiving itself. Through our ears, the universe is listening to its harmonies. We are the witnesses through which the universe becomes conscious of its glory, of its magnificence.

—*Alan W. Watts*

❧

A good garden may have some weeds.

—*Thomas Fuller*

Weeds are flowers, too, once you get to know them.

—*A.A. Milne*

Flowers remind me that life has its beautiful moments. My preference, though, is for wild flowers. Most things that will not be tamed are more appealing than those that are eager to please.

In winter dreams
Himalayan poppies bend
To the bracing wind,
And rhododendrons fling
Red petals at my feet.

Annie Powel. At the age of ninety, she was up early every morning to water her pretty little garden. Watering can in hand, she would move methodically from one flowerbed to the next, devotedly giving each plant a sprinkling. She said she loved to see leaves and flowers sparkling with fresh water; it gave her a new lease of life every day.

I used to visit and revisit [my garden] a dozen times a day, and stand in deep contemplation over my vegetable progeny with a love that nobody could share or conceive of who had never taken part in the process of creation. It was one of the most bewitching sights in the world to observe a hill of beans thrusting aside the soil, or a row of early peas just peeping forth sufficiently to trace a line of delicate green.

—*Nathaniel Hawthorne*

Beauty, the world seemed to say. And wherever he looked, at the houses, at the railings…beauty sprang instantly. To watch a leaf quivering in the rush of air was an exquisite joy. Up in the sky swallows swooping, swerving, flinging themselves in and out, round and round, yet always with perfect control as if elastics held them…and now again some chime (it might be a motor horn) tinkling divinely on the grass stalks—all of this, calm and reasonable as it was, made out of ordinary things as it was, was the truth now. Beauty was everywhere.

—*Virginia Woolf*

Notes

_____

_____

_____

_____

_____

_____

_____

_____

_____

_____

_____

_____

.78.

.Ruskin Bond.

_____
_____
_____
_____
_____
_____
_____
_____
_____
_____

_____
_____
_____
_____
_____
_____
_____
_____

.Ruskin Bond.

The most beautiful things in the world
cannot be seen or touched,
they are felt with the heart.

—Antoine de Saint-Exupéry

Whenever you are creating beauty around you, you are restoring your own soul.

—*Alice Walker*

❧

A cherry seed thrust without ceremony, without hope, into soft Himalayan earth. Four years later, it is taller than me, and sprinkled with pale pink blossoms in November.

❧

I rescued a dying asparagus fern from a neglected garden, and now, six months later, its strong feathery fronds have taken over most of my window, so that I have no need of curtains. And as the afternoon wanes, sunlight filters in green and mellow gold.

The setting sun spreads in the
    water
The river is half emerald, half red.
I love the third night of the
    ninth moon
The dew like pearls, the moon
    like a bow.
    —*Bai Juyi (tr. Sarah Beck)*

As to me, I know nothing else but miracles,
Whether I walk the streets of Manhattan,
Or dart my sight over the roofs of houses
　　toward the sky,
Or wade with naked feet along the beach
　　just in the edge of the water,
Or stand under the trees in the woods,
Or talk by day with any one I love,
Or sleep in bed at night with any one
　　I love…
The fishes that swim—the rocks—the
　　motion of the waves—the ships
　　with men in them,
What stranger miracles are there?
　　　—*Walt Whitman*

❧

That which is striking and beautiful
is not always good, but that which
is good is always beautiful.

—*Anne Ninon de L'Enclos*

Our hearts are drunk with a beauty
our eyes could never see.

—*George W. Russell*

I was walking through a stretch of wasteland, a desert that seemed to stretch endlessly. Just as the heat and the glare began to overwhelm me, I saw a tree. Just one small, crooked tree shimmering in the distance. And seeing it there all by itself, growing stubbornly where nothing else would, struggling on its own but giving hope and life to other things, was like finding a bit of heaven where I least expected it.

❧

The pure, the bright, the beautiful
That stirred our hearts in youth,
The impulse to a wordless prayer,
The dreams of love and truth;
The longings after something lost,
The spirit's yearning cry,
The striving after better hopes…
These things can never die.

.Ruskin Bond.

Notes

_.89._

🌿

.A Little Book of Beauty.

.90.

.Ruskin Bond.

_.91._

.Ruskin Bond.

The years have gone by,
   and sometimes I falter.
But still I set out for a stroll or a saunter,
   For the wind is as fresh
      as it was in my youth,
And the peach and the pear
      still the sweetest of fruit—
And the grass beneath my feet, still green.

The beauty or ugliness of a character lay not only in its achievements, but in its aims and impulses; its true history lay not among things done, but among things willed.

—*Thomas Hardy*

.94.

There are moments that come to each one of us, moments when we feel deeply moved or inspired, when time seems to stand still and we become acutely aware of the benediction of sun and wind and trees. Then heaven is here, compensating for the irritations and disasters that we build around ourselves each day.

Beauty itself is a painful convulsion in the heart, an abundance of vitality in the soul, and a mad chase undertaken by the spirit until it encounters the heavens.

—*Naguib Mahfouz*

Beauty can pierce one like a pain.

—*Thomas Mann*

Beauty is part of the finished language by which goodness speaks.

—*George Eliot*

Beauty awakens the soul to act.

—*Dante Alighieri*

Release the beauty in you in whatever way you see fit… We are elementally beautiful. In the hurry and strife of life we have grown away from the real thing. It just has to be restored to us. We must brush the ashes off and put roses in our hair.

—*Muriel Strode*

What humbugs we are, who pretend to live for Beauty, and never see the Dawn!

—*Logan Pearsall Smith*

A newlywed couple, barely adults, fall asleep at opposite ends of my bed. I curl up in my window seat. Nothing would induce me to disturb those innocents; they look so blissful in their slumbers.

If you have the ability, or rather the gift, of being able to see beauty in small things, then old age should hold no terrors.

Two memories of Shimla:

A sturdy little steam engine goes huffing and puffing through 103 tunnels. The rhododendrons have stained the slopes crimson with their blooms. A boy holding a lamb white as snow waves to me, and I wave back.

Standing on the Ridge at night, looking up through the clear air into the vault of the heavens where the stars seem so much nearer, wanting to whisper things to me. And they are reflected below, in the myriad lights of the shops and houses.

. R u s k i n   B o n d .

Notes

_____

_____

_____

_____

_____

_____

_____

_____

_____

_____

_____

_____

❧

.102.

.Ruskin Bond.

_____

_____

_____

_____

_____

_____

_____

_____

_____

_____   *.103.*

_____

_____

_____

_____

_____

_____

_____
_____
_____
_____
_____
_____
_____
_____
_____
_____
_____
_____
_____
_____
_____
_____
_____

.Ruskin Bond.

God grows weary of
  great kingdoms,
but never of little flowers.

—Rabindranath Tagore

If the path be beautiful let us not ask where it leads.

—*Anatole France*

Everybody needs beauty as well as bread, places to play in and pray in, where nature may heal and give strength to body and soul.

—*John Muir*

A monsoon afternoon, when the rain has stopped: a bright green snake suns itself on a rock, waiting for its hole to dry out.

❦

Outside the front door, a praying mantis reclining on a leaf of a honeysuckle creeper. Still young, a very tender pale green, like new leaves in the spring rain.

❦

Sometimes we are easily depressed by our surroundings, but we only need to look around us. The pebble at our feet, the wild flower growing out of rubble, dappled sunlight on a wall—they are as beautiful as any work of art.

❧

Even in the crowded city of flyovers and traffic jams there is the sky, there is sunrise and moonrise, there are birds, and people who smile.

❧

.Ruskin Bond.

By plucking her petals you do not gather the beauty of the flower.

—*Rabindranath Tagore*

❧

At some point in life the world's beauty becomes enough. You don't need to photograph, paint or even remember it. It is enough.

—*Toni Morrison*

❧

Beauty is in the heart of the beholder.

—*H.G. Wells*

The cosmos, tall and erect, its foliage uncomplicated, its sky-blue inflorescence bold and cheerful: the genius of simplicity.

A flower blossoms for its own joy.
—*Oscar Wilde*

I do not have much patience with a thing of beauty that must be explained to be understood. If it does need additional interpretation by someone other than the creator, then I question whether it has fulfilled its purpose.
—*Charlie Chaplin*

That which is not slightly distorted lacks sensible appeal; from which it follows that irregularity—that is to say, the unexpected, surprise and astonishment—are an essential part and characteristic of beauty.

—*Charles Baudelaire*

You don't have to be perfect to be pretty.

—*Carson Kressley*

Notes

_____
_____
_____
_____
_____
_____
_____
_____
_____
_____
_____
_____
_____

❧

.114.

.Ruskin Bond.

_.115._

_____

_____

_____

_____

_____

_____

_____

_____

_____

_____

_____

_____

_____

_____

_____

_____

_____

.Ruskin Bond.

Enough for me that you walk past,
A firefly flashing in the dark.

In the silence that settles in the hills at night, the smallest sounds become clear—a field mouse rustling through dry leaves, a seed falling, and the drip of the dew running off the roof. And if I am lucky, I hear something that makes no sound at all but draws me to my window, to see the moon coming up silently over the deodars.

.Ruskin Bond.

There are sounds that come from a distance, beautiful because they are far away, voices on the wind, voices through space: The cries of fishermen out on the river. Drums beating rhythmically in a distant village. A woman, somewhere high up on a hill, calling out to her cows to come home. The music of a flute from the depths of a valley. The voice of a long-departed friend on the telephone, from oceans away.

❧

Listen to the night wind in the
   trees,
Listen to the summer grass singing;
Listen to the moon as it climbs
   the sky,
Listen to the pebbles humming;
Listen to the mist in the trembling
   leaves,

Listen to the silence calling.

Life seems to go on without effort
when I am filled with music.
   —*George Eliot*

Real poetry is to lead a beautiful
life. To live poetry is better than
to write it.

—*Matsuo Basho*

I have nature and art and poetry,
and if that is not enough, what is
enough?

—*Vincent van Gogh*

In the thrill of little leaves
I see the air's invisible dance,
And in their glimmering
The secret heart-beats of the sky.

—*Rabindranath Tagore*

Three o'clock in the morning. The soft April night is looking at my windows and caressingly winking at me with its stars. I can't sleep, I am so happy.

—*Anton Chekhov*

Real strength never impairs beauty or harmony, but it often bestows it, and in everything imposingly beautiful, strength has much to do with the magic.

—*Herman Melville*

Perhaps all the dragons in our lives are princesses who are only waiting to see us act, just once, with beauty and courage.

—*Rainer Maria Rilke*

…he that dares not grasp the thorn should never crave the rose.

—*Anne Bronte*

There is no excellent beauty that hath not some strangeness in the proportion.

—*Francis Bacon*

Notes

_____

_____

_____

_____

_____

_____

_____

_____

_____

_____

_____

_____

_____

❧

.126.

_____
_____
_____
_____
_____
_____
_____
_____
_____
_____
_____
_____
_____
_____
_____

_.127._

.128.

🌱

.Ruskin Bond.

Your head is a living forest
full of songbirds.

—e.e. cummings

Is it so small a thing
To have enjoyed the sun
To have lived light in the spring
To have loved, to have thought, to
have done?
—*Matthew Arnold*

That love of my youth—a distant memory now, but a bright one, like a forget-me-not blooming on a bare rock.

Why be ashamed of nostalgia? It is simply an attempt to try and preserve that which was good and beautiful in the past. It might even improve the present!

Do I love you because you're
    beautiful,
Or are you beautiful because I
    love you?
    —*Richard Rodgers and Oscar*
    Hammerstein II

Between our two lives
there is also the life of
the cherry blossom.
    —*Matsuo Basho (tr. Sam Hamill)*

Your face streamed April rain,
As you climbed the steep hill…
Your feet, laved with dew,
Stood firm on the quickening
    grass.
There was a butterfly between us:
Red and gold its wings
And heavy with dew.

.133.

Jasmine flowers in her hair,
Languid summer days are here,
And sweet longing scents the air.

The Whistler, carefree, easy-going, always whistling—loudly and tunefully (a bird turned into a boy!)—so that you know when he's coming round a bend or through the trees. And if you turn to look, he smiles, and you forget your troubles.

Nothing can make our life, or the lives of other people, more beautiful than perpetual kindness.

—Leo Tolstoy

I wish I could show you when
you are lonely or in darkness the
astonishing light of your own
being.

—*Hafiz*

❧

For a day, just for one day,
Talk about that which disturbs
    no one
And bring some peace into your
    beautiful eyes.

—*Hafiz*

❧

Avoid mirrors as far as possible. You might need a mirror for shaving, or dabbing a little something of whatever it is that must be dabbed on your face; but afterwards, put it away and try looking at the world instead—the contours are far more interesting.

No spring nor summer beauty hath such grace as I have seen in one autumnal face.

—*John Donne*

.Ruskin Bond.

Notes

_____
_____
_____
_____
_____
_____
_____
_____
_____
_____
_____
_____
_____

_____

_____

_____

_____

_____

_____

_____

_____

_____

_____

_____

_____

_____

_____

_____

_____

.Ruskin Bond.

_____

_____

_____

_____

_____

_____

_____

_____

_____   *.139.*

_____

_____

_____

_____

_____

_____

_____

❧

❧

.Ruskin Bond.

Earth's crammed with heaven
And every common bush afire with God:
But only he who sees takes off his shoes...

—Elizabeth Barret Browning

One of the most tragic things I know about human nature is that all of us tend to put off living. We are all dreaming of some magical rose garden over the horizon instead of enjoying the roses that are blooming outside our windows today.

—*Dale Carnegie*

There's a little waterfall in my hills. The sun strikes it from behind an overhanging rock and creates a tiny, tenuous rainbow. I bathe beneath the rainbow. I stretch out on the grass. The sun bathes everything with clear, warm light and above me, a pair of dragonflies hover, crossing and re-crossing the air in a dance of love.

I have erred so unremittingly in my fallacious conception of utility. I will look upon the rose gardens whose use is beauty…I knew that I must plant my fields to save my body, but did I not know that I must plant my rose gardens to save my soul?

—*Muriel Strode*

Know, son, that everything in the
universe is a pitcher brimming
with wisdom and beauty; the
universe is a drop of the 'Tigris of
His beauty.

—*Rumi (tr. Andrew Harvey)*

Ghalib, it is the rose's beauty that
    teaches us to gaze.
No matter what the scene, no one
Should ever close his eyes.

—*Mirza Ghalib (tr. Ralph Russell)*

may my heart always be open to
    little
birds who are the secrets of living
whatever they sing is better than
    to know
and if men should not hear them
    men are old

—*e.e. cummings*

🌿

The lovely flowers embarrass me.
They make me regret I am not a
bee.

—*Emily Dickinson*

🌿

The first snowfall of the winter. The deodars at the top of the hill are clothed in a mantle of white. It is a fairyland, everything still and silent. The only movement is the circling of an eagle over the trees.

❧

A winter gift: a lone fox dancing in the bright moonlight. I pull my coat around me and watch from the shadows. All things bright and beautiful…

❧

We need beauty because it makes
us ache to be worthy of it.
    —*Mary Oliver*

Beauty is eternity gazing at itself
    in a mirror.
But you are eternity and you are
    the mirror.
        —*Kahlil Gibran*

Notes

_____

_____

_____

_____

_____

_____

_____   *.149.*

_____

_____

_____

_____

_____

_____

_____

❧

.Ruskin Bond.

_.151._

___

.Ruskin Bond.

When love is constant,
beauty is infinite.

The sudden desire to look beautiful made her straighten her back. Beautiful? For whom? Why, for myself, of course.

—*Colette*

As long as I love Beauty I am young.

—*William Henry Davies*

Beauty is in the eye of the beholder:
A wild rose bush growing out of
an old car in a junkyard.

The snows are melting in the
high mountains. In our hills, the
grass, straw-yellow in winter, is
now green and sweet, sprinkled
with buttercups and clover.

.155.

Peace is always beautiful.
—*Walt Whitman*

Three things cause sorrow to flee: water, green trees and a beautiful face.
—*Moroccan proverb*

Monsoon in the hills: The swish of rain on tin roofs. The slopes are a lush green, thick with ferns and wild flowers. The mist trails up the valleys. The call of the kastura can be heard in every glen.

❧

Spring in the hills: The honeybees push their way through the pursed lips of the pink and violet antirrhinum and disappear completely. A few minutes later they stagger out, bottoms first.

❧

Beauty! What can be said of it? What is it? I look around, to see some object especially beautiful, on which to expend my panegyrics. There is the deep fathomless azure above me; there is the sea, the wild, open, careering ocean; there is a fair girl, a beautiful boy; there are the stars looking down from heaven; there is beauty in the human countenance, beauty in looks, beauty in thoughts, beauty in actions. What shall I say! I am bewildered; beauty overwhelms me.

—*T.C. Henley*

Always try to keep a patch of sky
above your life.

—*Marcel Proust*

And the most beautiful moments,
dear reader, the most beautiful
dreams, are those that we can share.

Ruskin Bond is the author of numerous novellas, short-story collections and non-fiction books, many of them classics. Among them are *The Room on the Roof*, *A Flight of Pigeons*, *The Night Train at Deoli*, *Time Stops at Shamli*, *Rain in the Mountains*, *A Book of Simple Living* and his autobiography, *Lone Fox Dancing*. He received the Sahitya Akademi Award in 1993, the Padma Shri in 1999 and the Padma Bhushan in 2014. He lives in Landour, Mussoorie, with his extended family.

www.ingramcontent.com/pod-product-compliance
Lightning Source LLC
Chambersburg PA
CBHW051325050726
47504CB00014B/1864